I LIKE TO PLAY AND WIN!

THE STORY OF A SOCCER PLAYER

Massase Abraham

I LIKE TO PLAY AND WIN!
THE STORY OF A SOCCER PLAYER

iUniverse books may be ordered through booksellers or by contacting:

iUniverse
1663 Liberty Drive
Bloomington, IN 47403
www.iuniverse.com
1-800-Authors (1-800-288-4677)

Because of the dynamic nature of the Internet, any web addresses or links contained in this book may have changed since publication and may no longer be valid. The views expressed in this work are solely those of the author and do not necessarily reflect the views of the publisher, and the publisher hereby disclaims any responsibility for them.

Any people depicted in stock imagery provided by Getty Images are models, and such images are being used for illustrative purposes only.
Certain stock imagery © Getty Images.

ISBN: 978-1-5320-5361-0 (sc)
ISBN: 978-1-5320-5362-7 (e)

Library of Congress Control Number: 2018909949

Print information available on the last page.

iUniverse rev. date: 08/30/2018

CONTENTS

CHAPTER ONE:
Introduction to Soccer

"Da...da..." Massi called as he crawled along the floor to his father. John Dearson crouched so that he was eye level with his child.

"Come to papa Massi. Come on, you can do it."

Massi was a year and a half but he still didn't talk very well. He liked to follow his dad everywhere though and do everything his father did. Today his father was going to play soccer with his pals from the neighborhood. Massi clung to him, not wanting to be left behind.

"Aww, you wanna go with papa to play ball huh?" John said giving his son a pleased smile. He loved that his son loved to spend time with him.

"John you can't go with Massi. Who will watch him while you play?" Melissa, John's wife and Massi's mother called.

"I was thinking you could come with us too." John called back with a cheeky smile.

Melissa sighed, "I'd love to dear, you know that. But who would make dinner if I went?"

"Oh don't worry about dinner. We'll stop by Alfredo's Diner and get something to eat on the way home. I think the special is lasagna tonight," John said excitedly. He loved Alfredo's lasagna.

"Okay then," Melissa said with a smile, "I'll get our things together."

∞

"Tha! Tha!" Massi exclaimed throwing his hands up in the air excitedly as he watched his father run on the field passing the ball to his teammates. His mother stood him up on her lap so he could dance around even more excitedly as he watched the game.

"I take it you like soccer," she said to him in amusement.

"Tha!" Massi replied jumping up and down in her lap, his short fat legs kicking out in imitation of his father.

Once the game was over, Melissa put Massi on the ground so he could toddle over to his waiting dad. Massi bypassed John and headed straight for the soccer ball.

"Oh, you want to play big guy?" John said with a laugh, following his son closely.

"Tha!" Massi said slapping ineffectually at the ball.

John stood him up and took hold of his leg, "You wanna learn how to kick?" he asked his toddler.

"Da!" Massi said.

So John gently bent Massi's leg and then swung it forward so it hit the ball. The ball rolled a few inches and John cheered loudly.

"You did it Massi! You kicked the ball."

"Aaaaah!" Massi said jumping up and down in joy.

John helped Massi to kick the ball around a few more times before Melissa declared it was time to leave. John picked Massi off the ground and followed his wife to the car after waving good-bye to his teammates.

∞

Alfredo's Diner tasted particularly sublime that evening. Massi got sauce all over his face and shirt but Melissa had it covered with a change of clothes in her bag and wet wipes. They stopped by a soccer shop on their way home and bought a tiny soccer ball, small enough for Massi to play with. He jumped up and down with excitement when he saw it, keeping up a running commentary of excitable chatter all the way home before crashing hard just before they arrived home.

"He's asleep," Melissa whispered as the car came to a stop, "You think I should wake him up for his bath?"

John shook his head, "let him sleep. He can bathe in the morning." He whispered back.

Melissa was skeptical but then she thought about how grumpy Massi got if you woke him up before he was ready and decided to go along with her husband's suggestion. They put him to bed in his room, his new soccer ball awaiting him in the corner.

Massi's absolute new favorite toy was the soccer ball. He woke up in the morning and instead of going in search of Melissa to wake her up, he ran to the corner, picked up his ball and put it on the ground. Then he began to kick it while laughing with glee. Melissa was woken by his hoots of laughter and when she went to check on him, he was running after his ball, which had spilled out onto the corridor and was bouncing toward the stairs.

She quickly hurried forward, picking up the ball before it could roll down the stairs then turned and picked Massi up before he could begin to protest.

"That's the last time you sleep with your bedroom door open young man," she said, heart still beating fast at the thought of him falling down the stairs.

"John!" she called as she stepped into the kitchen.

"Yes dear?" he said coming into the kitchen while straightening his tie.

"We need to put a stair gate at the top of the stairs." Melissa informed him.

"Okay dear, I will take care of it after church," he said as he kissed her forehead and then Massi's, "What happened, little Massi make a break for it?" he asked as he grinned at his son.

"He was going to follow his new favorite toy down the stairs," she said holding up the ball.

"Oh" John said eyes lighting up with delight, "You really like soccer don't you Massi?" he said bumping his nose against Massi's.

"Aah!" Massi said and John took that as agreement.

∞

Massi joined his father every week at soccer practice. As his father played on the pitch, he practiced with his tiny ball on the sidelines, copying every move he saw.

"You have a future champ there," one of the other mothers told Melissa as they watched Massi practice.

"Thanks," Melissa said smiling hard, "he really enjoys it. Wants to be just like his father."

The lady smiled as they continued to watch Massi kicking the ball. A bigger boy came by, wanting to play with him but Massi wasn't having it. Every time the bigger boy tried to steal the ball from him, Massi would parry and deflect, kicking it away from him.

"Wow he's good." John's friend said watching the little exchange.

"Really?" Melissa asked.

"Very good," their friend replied, "How old is he?"

"He's just under two years old," Melissa said.

"You nurture that talent he could go far."

∞

Massi continued to get better as he got older, gaining more ball control, learning to weave and run with it. His legs got stronger and steadier as he grew older and he kept practicing alone and with his dad. Sometimes Melissa would ask the neighborhood kids over for a match. They would play in the backyard, three a side, with two mothers serving as goalkeepers; and Massi's team always won.

"Massi is really good at the sport," the other mothers told Melissa, "Maybe you should enroll him in a little league."

"Don't you think it's too early? He's barely a toddler," Melissa would reply.

"I'm sure you can find a toddler team for him to play with. Obviously our kids are outclassed,"

the other mothers said good naturedly.

Melissa waited for John to get home so she could talk it over with him.

"Hey should we enroll Massi in a little soccer league?" She asked as she cleared the plates after dinner.

"I don't know. Should we?" John asked, putting down the paper, "I don't want to be one of those parents who enroll their kids in all kinds of activities and put undue pressure on them."

"Okay but see the other parents say that Massi's too good to play with their kids now. That maybe we should get him in a team where he can feel challenged."

"Mmm," John said thoughtfully, "It's something to think about. Could you find out if there is a kids league nearby please darling?"

"Okay, I will."

"Thank you."

∞

Melissa made inquiries and to her surprise she did find a soccer league for kids not too far from their home. It was more like a play group than a sports team but they had small goal posts and a marked field, about an eighth of the size of a real soccer field; they also had coaches and uniforms. It was all very cute and Melissa was charmed. When she brought Massi for a look see, he took one look at the other kids playing and shot off to join them.

Melissa laughed, shrugging helplessly at the coach.

"I'm guessing that means we should say 'welcome to the club'," the coach said with a pleased smile.

"Yes please," Melissa said.

So every Tuesday and Thursday Melissa or John brought Massi to learn the basics of soccer at the little league. Massi couldn't understand why he couldn't go *every day* and tended to throw up quite a fuss.

"Want to play!" he would cry and Melissa would hand him his ball and ask him to go and play with Josh from next door.

"Mo mo mo! Want to play in league," he would say with a huge pout on his face.

"Tomorrow you can go. Today they're not there," his mother tried to explain but Massi just wasn't getting it.

"Okay Massi," John said scooping him up off the ground, "How about you come and play with your daddy. You like playing with daddy right?"

Massi gave him a huge smile and they went into the backyard and kicked the ball around while Melissa watched from the window with a smile.

Massi really loved soccer. She could see that for herself. It was a great bond between father and son but also hopefully Massi would be able to live his passion and turn it into something great.

Melissa sighed, "Fingers crossed," she said to herself as she watched her son lob the wall way over his father's head.

"Should he be able to do that already?" she murmured to herself, "I don't think his legs are supposed to be strong enough."

She watched for a bit as her husband acted as goalie and Massi lobbed two balls past him into 'goal'.

"That's my boy!" she exclaimed loudly enough for them to hear as she clapped for him. Massi shot his hands in the air and did a victory dance as his parents laughed with delight.

CHAPTER TWO:
Kindergarten

Massi joined kindergarten at five years old. Melissa and John were careful to choose one with a vigorous sports program because every minute of every day, Massi wanted to be playing soccer. His parents supported him in his need to play but set a strict schedule just so he wouldn't forget to eat and sleep.

The kindergarten they took him to was in a diverse neighborhood and he came across boys and girls of many different backgrounds. He made friends easily because he was a happy kid who just wanted to share his love for soccer. Every day he would put on his blue and red Barcelona soccer shirt with Massi printed along the back along with the number ten, together with the matching shorts. He wore his long socks and soccer cleats and then had his breakfast.

His mother would make him cereal or sometimes porridge and he made sure to eat all of it because his mother said it would make him big and strong and better able to play. After breakfast his dad would wait with him in the yard for the school bus while they kicked his - slightly bigger – soccer ball around.

Once the school bus came he would jump on it excitedly greeting everyone before going to sit with his friends, Aja and Singh. They would catch each other up on what they did the day before after school was let out, and then talk about soccer teams and which ones they wanted to join when they were big enough.

Massi always said Barcelona or Chelsea. He wasn't sure which one yet. All he knew was that he wanted to play soccer forever. Once the bus reached the school, they would all jump out and put their bags in their lockers before assembly. The day would begin with singing and announcements and then every class went off to learn and play for the rest of the day.

At lunchtimes, when everyone had eaten and they were allowed to go outside to play, Massi would organize his friends into two teams. It was hard because everyone wanted to be on his team since he was the best player. Other kids were mean and said things like.

"You think you're the only one who knows how to play soccer?"

Or try to push him into the dirt and laugh at him. Massi just ignored them. They were just jealous that they couldn't play as well as him.

After they chose teams, the designated referee would blow the whistle and they would start the game. Massi was good at ball control and weaving his way through defenders to score a goal. It was like when he was in the zone, the only things he could see were the ball and his path. And he knew just where to tap to take the ball where he needed it to be, tap again to avoid a defender coming at him, kick it a bit and do a run to get past two defenders coming from both sides, then a clear run to the goal post. It was just him, and the goalkeeper now. He would zig and zag, feint to the right and then kick the ball with his left. The goalie would scramble for it, but too late! The ball had already hit the net. Score!

Massi jumped up and down, running to the side of the pitch and skidding to the end on his knees while his teammates piled on top of it. He almost enjoyed the celebrating more than the game. Then it was back to defending, making sure the other team didn't score either. Massi was good at both attack and defense so he played in the midfield, so he could do both. He kept an eye out for his teammates, making sure they were doing what they were supposed to too. His chest was heaving with exertion and he was having the time of his life. Then the bell rang for class and they all scattered back to their classrooms.

This was their routine day in and day out. His friends Aja and Singh always refused to play, saying that Massi got very emotional during matches and they didn't want to fight with him. He accepted it but he was sad that his close friends didn't want to play with him. When they moved up to elementary school he met Thomas who transferred to their school from out of state. Thomas was from Texas and he really liked beef. That put Singh off and he said a couple of rude things to Thomas. Thomas was surprised by Singh's rudeness because he hadn't meant anything by it and it became a huge fight with Aja and Massi in the middle trying to keep the peace. Eventually Thomas ran off to sit by himself in the corner.

"Um, Thomas?" Massi said as he came tentatively up to him after story time.

Thomas turned from stacking pillows to find Massi standing behind him.

"Yes?"

"I really...I wanted to say sorry for Singh. He listens to his mom, and that's what she believes right? Don't be mad at him?"

Turning back to the pillows, Thomas said, "He can think whatever he wants. It's not my business."

From across the classroom, Aja called, "You don't have to stack those! The teacher will do it."

Thomas ignored her.

"Don't be mad at him. Please." Thomas glanced back over his shoulder. "He's my friend, and so are you. I don't like you being mad at each other."

Thomas shrugged. "He said what he said and so did I".

"All right." Massi paused, and Thomas acted like the conversation was finished. "I was wondering..."

Thomas said, "Yes?"

"Um. Well I noticed you were watching at lunchtime, and I thought maybe... would you like to learn soccer?"

"Well, I don't know..."

"Aja and Singh never play..."

"Oh." Thomas thought about it. "Okay."

"Good." Massi smiled suddenly, unexpectedly. "Talk to you about it later, then."

"All right."

Massi smiled again and went back to his other friends. Thomas blinked and returned to stacking the pillows.

∞

"This is the ball..." Massi kicked it towards Thomas.

Thomas picked the ball up; it was white, with red lines connecting the hexagonal panels. "I thought they were black and white."

"They were. Now, they make many different colors. And put it down—you're not allowed to use your hands."

Thomas dropped the ball and toed it towards Massi.

"That's the first thing—never use your toes. You can break them, or deform them. My dad told me that. Lots of soccer players end up needing toe surgery. Use the inside of your foot, like this." He turned his foot sideways, so his toe was pointing almost straight out to his side, and gently kicked the ball in Thomas's direction.

"Your turn."

Turning his foot, Thomas scuffed the ball in Massi's general direction. Massi cracked a smile. "Well, not bad...you didn't play when you were younger, right?"

"No."

"Not bad, then. Here, try again."

Thomas managed to get the ball within two feet of Massi this time. Massi easily sidestepped and did something with his foot to make the ball roll softly to where he'd been standing.

"That's passing," he said. "Passing you do between two people, like this. Dribbling is what you do when you want to run with the ball...you turn your foot the other way, like this," he directed his left toe to point more or less towards his right instep, "and push the ball with the outside edge of your foot. Okay? Like this."

He kicked the ball in a few short steps over to where Thomas was standing. "Try it."

Thomas dribbled at a more or less forty-five degree angle to where he was intending to go.

"Well...close. Again."

This time, Thomas made less of an angle, though he ended up a few feet away from Massi.

"Okay, better," Massi said. "Pass it again..."

Thomas did.

"All right..." Massi passed it back "...so now dribble again..."

They continued for a few more minutes.

"You really love this, don't you?" Thomas asked.

"Always played with the kids on my street since I was younger. They're good memories."

"I suppose so."

Massi trapped the ball again and met Thomas's eyes with a grin. "But now we get to the fun part of soccer."

"Which is?"

"Keep away!" Massi said, kicking the ball and sprinting after it. "Come on, Thomas! Try to get the ball away from me!"

Thomas went sprinting after Massi, who was even faster dribbling the soccer ball than simple running.

After they'd finished and washed up in the school bathroom, Massi asked, "Did you have fun?"

Emphatically, Thomas said, "Yes!"

"Want to try again sometime, then?"

"Of course."

"Good. Next week, then?"

∞

After four weeks, Thomas finally managed to steal the ball away from Massi. Massi immediately came close to knocking him over with a shoulder before getting the ball right back.

"Hey!" said Thomas.

"Perfectly legal," Massi said. "I didn't actually push you or trip you or grab your clothes or anything."

"So I can just run into you any time I want?"

"As long as you're going for the ball."

"Sounds good," Thomas said, before launching himself against Massi's side and taking the ball back.

"Oh, you want to play dirty, eh?"

Thomas only grinned.

∞

A few weeks later, Massi had to drag Thomas out to the open space they used as a pitch. There was a deep chill in the air, but Massi seemed determined. Thomas's mind wasn't really on the game, though, and he missed Massi on every pass for about five minutes.

"You're not paying attention," Massi said.

"Sorry," Thomas said, surly.

"No, you're not," Massi said. "You're feeling sorry for yourself because our team beat your team last time we played."

"Well, how would *you* feel if you had been practicing as much as I and you got beat five nil?"

"I would feel terrible; but you were playing against me so it shouldn't surprise you that you lost."

"Well, that's different."

"Different how?"

"Well, for one thing, we should have at least been able to score one goal!"

"That's true," Massi said. "But you just started playing a few weeks ago. You're really pretty good. You'll score a goal soon."

"Yeah okay, but when?" Thomas said. He wished very much he still had the ball, which was currently at rest under Massi's left foot; scuffing it in Massi's direction would illustrate his point rather nicely.

"Soon. I promise."

Thomas frowned. "You can't know that."

"Well, yes I can because I've been teaching you."

"Oh."

"So, keep playing soccer with me?" Massi's smile was playful now, daring. "It'll keep you in shape..."

"Maybe," Thomas said resentfully.

"Then catch me!" Massi ran off quickly, and Thomas sprinted to keep up. He felt justified when Massi ended up in the grass, and pretended his elbow had nothing to do with it.

∞

"Orange?" Thomas asked incredulously as they walked out of the school.

"So we can see it in the snow," Massi explained.

"When did it snow?!?"

"This afternoon, didn't you see?"

"No I had a makeup class with the math teacher..."

"Again?"

"Yeah."

Massi set off dribbling a quick circle around Thomas; Thomas admired the way his legs moved, even hampered by their thick winter clothing. "You're really very good at that," he said.

Massi's feet did a complicated dance with the ball as Thomas whistled.

"Thanks," Massi said.

"My pleasure."

Doing something complicated with his feet again, Massi managed to twist the ball in Thomas's direction. Thomas stopped it—trapped; he reminded himself—and sent it rolling back.

∞

As he dribbled out onto the "pitch" with the white and red ball, Thomas had a sudden thought.

"Massi?"

"Yeah?" Massi puffed, bouncing up and down on his toes.

"Where do you keep the orange ball in the summer?"

"In my family garage, obviously," Massi said.

Thomas waited.

"Oh, you were trying to be funny!"

"Thanks...."

"No. That's good!"

"Just get on with it," Thomas said. "All right. Well, today, I'm going to teach you to tackle!"

"Tackle?" Thomas asked, "I know what a tackle is."

"Not that kind, stupid. It's how you take the ball off people."

"Oh. That wouldn't've helped at keep away at all, oh no."

"Well. You just get up close to the other player, right, and when he stops to make a move, you just scoop the ball away. Or if its right up against his foot, you hit as hard as you can with your foot on the other side, and either it'll go spinning away and you can get it, or it'll knock him over and you get the ball anyway."

"Sounds painful."

"Oh, it is. Want to try?"

They got very dirty again that day especially since the spring rains had made the ground soft and muddy.

∞

"What made *you* so happy?" Thomas asked.

"We beat the Spurs! One-nil! A shutout! On their home pitch!" Massi was practically dancing, the ball moving with him.

"Shutout?" Thomas asked. "Spurs? We?"

"Barcelona! Obviously!" now Massi was nearly *singing*. "We beat the Spurs! One-nil! They got *no goals!* This is so great!"

"We won, we won, we won..."

Thomas exclaimed, "Well...I'm happy for you?"

"Thanks!" Massi grinned blindingly.

∞

May dawned bright and warm. Their little corner of grass was relatively secluded, though, so they could practice in peace.

"Why did you ask me to do this, anyway?" Thomas asked.

"Because soccer is a metaphor for life," Massi intoned seriously.

"Spare me," Thomas said, grabbing his heart.

"Good, because I don't know how it's a metaphor. I just heard my dad say that one Thursday at practice." Massi was doing something impressive he called juggling; the ball hadn't touched the ground in probably a minute. Thomas watched, enthralled.

"Besides," he added, "this way I always win."

"Hey!"

"It's true. Oh, crap," Massi said as the ball dropped to the ground. "Anyway— here, you try—" he kicked the ball over, "why did you agree?"

"Don't know," Thomas said, mostly concentrating on keeping the ball in the air for more than one kick. "Sounded like fun?"

"Right," Massi said. "You just wanted to get away from Aja and Singh."

"No...Maybe it was those big, puppy-dog eyes."

"Oh really?"

"Yes. You looked so sorry when you asked me."

"Those big, puppy-dog eyes are going to steal the ball from you," Massi said, and did just that.

∞

"Come on, tackle me!" Massi taunted, pulling the ball away at the last second.

Again.

Thomas pushed his foot forward, only to be thwarted again. "I would if you'd let me!" he finally exploded.

"You can do it, Thomas!"

"Can't," Thomas muttered, and kicked at the ball rather violently. It knocked against, then through, Massi's foot as he dribbled towards Thomas; he fell forward, into Thomas, knocking him slightly over.

"Told you," he said, with a grin of surprisingly white teeth, from this angle anyway. He pushed himself up, and then offered a hand to Thomas.

Thomas glared.

"Right. Well. Perhaps...perhaps long passes."

"All right."

CHAPTER THREE:
Elementary School

Grade three was a very hard year for Massi. Halfway through the summer before the academic year started, Massi's home team was disbanded because half the kids were away at camp. He wasn't able to play except with Thomas.

Melissa and John continued to encourage Massi to practice at home his skills. During these times they were able to spend with their offspring and, as a family, partook in different sports. When his family had started to play soccer, it was like Massi had found his calling. He had taken to the sport like a fish to water. He was then working hard to improve his skills and become the best player he could.

∞

Massi was, by nature, a shy yet friendly person, and he had friends not only on the school team but also several opposing teams. As practice began, Massi grew more and more popular with the school team because of his skill and teamwork. Massi was so kind and sincere to everyone regardless of how they looked or acted, which together with his skills made him a team and coach favorite. He wasn't greedy with his talents either, kindly sharing with anyone who asked for his help.

The soccer players had also liked Massi for another reason too. When Massi put his cleats on, it was like he became a completely different person. While Massi was usually a shy person, when he took the field, he was fierce, aggressive, and occasionally feared by those weak of heart. There was also a joke that had surfaced shortly after the team saw the other side of Massi that when he sprinted down the sideline after the ball, he slightly resembled a soaring eagle hunting down its prey. After that was mentioned, the nickname of "Soaring Eagle" was permanently stuck to Massi.

Soon enough, Coach Asher realized Massi is a good player and that he could grow even more. Massi was given the position center-mid; and in his second season got to play number 10 in the team. He became one of the coach's best players and Massi always listened very carefully to him. He made many friends in the team, and sometimes friends from the opponent teams. Massi was very open to learning from other good players, from the coach, and continued to learn from his dad. Massi is not selfish when playing soccer. His mom yelled at him one time from the side as she was watching the game "Score Massi, score!" But Massi answered "Coach told me it's an easy game, I just have to pass the ball". He let others score. It was so much fun to watch, such a great team.

Other times at a game someone slide tackled him and hit Massi's ankle with his cleats causing a bruise. He ran for the ball, trying not to put too much weight on his ankle, but also trying not to let anyone see how much pain he was in. The two teams were tied with only a few minutes to go in the game and Massi really, really wanted his team to win. It wasn't that he was especially competitive – it didn't actually bother him all that much whether he *personally* won or lost – but Frank Smith, the captain of the local soccer team, had been putting all his time and energy into the team ever since Coach Asher had given him the position at the beginning of the season. Massi was not going to let him down by ducking out of the game now.

In the beginning, the coaches had seen him play during his lunchtime matches with his classmates and friends and recruited him for the elementary school soccer team. He wasn't a fan of cutthroat competition although he did like winning. For him it was all about the teamwork. Still, his dad had said it would be good for him to get into competitive sports and really measure his skills against other equally skilled people. So Massi had agreed to join the soccer team a little over a year and a half ago now. His first real competitive game was nerve wracking.

"Pass Massi!" Thomas hollered as Massi ran up the field, ball in tow. He quickly passed it to Tom who kicked it right to the back of the net.

Right after that amazing goal, the whistle blew, and the game was over. The elementary school team roared with pride and the crowd cheered as if there was no tomorrow. And why wouldn't they? They were through to the final.

"Good game boys." Frank cheered as they walked into the changing rooms, high-fiving all the boys as he passed.

"And give it up for our amazing captain, Mr. Frank Smith!" Massi hollered. Another cheer erupted from the small room as they chanted the name of their leader.

Then the coach, Mr. Asher Roberts walked in.

"Brilliant game boys!" He exclaimed in happiness. "Especially you four!" He said pointing to Massi, Andrew, Thomas and Frank.

"Thanks Mr. Roberts!" Massi chirped, beaming with pride. At 9, Massi was the youngest on the intermediate team.

"So now boys, we just need to see what we're up against! Anyone up for a little trip to see the other teams match tomorrow, see who gets through and all?" Frank called. All of the boys responded with a collective yes so that was it.

Tomorrow, they were going to league intermediate.

Singh had laughed when Massi had hidden in his bedroom after the first match was over, wide eyed and whispering secrets about the difference between playing for fun and playing for competition. About the captain who was in the grade above with the green eyes and the freckles who had been so *nice* to Massi when he'd fallen over in the mud, who had helped him up with his big strong hands and who had yelled at two other, even bigger boys in the locker rooms. After, they'd been talking loudly about which new kids had potential and which didn't. Who had offered him candy and someone to wait with after he saw that Massi's parents were late picking him up.

"Why Massi, I didn't expect that your excitement about soccer could get any deeper," Singh smirked after Massi had told him how excited he was to go back next week.

"It's not deeper; it's just that these guys are really serious. The coach is really serious about the team," Massi insisted.

"You sure?" Singh teased. "You're sure you can handle the pressure?"

"Of course!" Massi sulked, and Singh just smiled knowingly.

When Coach Asher announced the team list for the league game today, and Massi heard his own name being called, Frank had nudged him in the ribs and Massi had wondered if he was ready for this. Frank was allowed to help with the team list, and there were definitely boys who Massi thought might be better than him who hadn't been picked. He tentatively asked Frank about it after practice.

"I didn't make him pick you, Massi. You've never played a league game before, I guess Coach Asher wanted to give you a chance to prove yourself. You know you've been playing really well in practice," had been Frank's response.

"That's stupid. What if I mess up and we lose? It'll be my fault because someone better than me could have played," Massi countered.

"You won't mess up, you'll do great," Frank had tried to reassure him, rubbing a hand on his back for a moment. "We can practice more this afternoon if you like."

They had practiced that afternoon, for as long as Massi could stand until he was too tired to even see the ball, and then they'd hidden in Frank's room and watched this hospital program on TV that Mrs. Smith said was 'too grown-up for them' but that neither Frank nor Massi could get enough of, until Massi fell asleep on the couch, exhausted. Massi had practiced every day that week too, both before and after school, doing everything he could to avoid letting the team down; letting his coaches and captain down.

"Frank thinks I can do it, so I can," Massi had whispered to himself that morning as he was pulling on his shoes.

He'd pretended he wasn't nervous all through warm ups, just trying not to look like an easy target to the other team. He'd managed to look all the members of the opposition in the eye as he shook their hands before the game, and in the first half he'd stayed mostly off to the side, out of the center of the action. He didn't come into contact with the ball, but he was there, ready to back anybody up if they needed him, hoping it looked like he was doing something useful. Melissa and John were in the crowd, cheering away for him. He didn't want to let them down either.

It was a little after half time that it happened. Andrew, one of Massi's teammates, had the ball, but he was surrounded by a knot of other players and it would be difficult for him to keep possession for long. Massi was on the sidelines, a little further from the goal but completely alone. Andrew saw the opportunity and kicked the ball as hard as he could towards Massi, and somehow, completely unexpectedly, Massi didn't miss. He stumbled a little and struggled to get going but a moment later he was off dribbling the ball towards the goal.

Only, in doing so he'd had to cut across the path of the group, fast catching up to him, and even though he'd tried to kick the ball away from them, he hadn't been quick enough to stop himself tripping over another boy's foot, sprawling on the grass with a sudden shooting pain in his ankle.

Massi felt tears stinging his eyes and forced himself not to reach out and grab his leg. He knew he'd be allowed to step out if he said something to Coach Asher, but now that he was here, he wanted to see this through.

He didn't want Frank to see him as the boy who couldn't even survive one whole game without having to take a break.

He'd tried to avoid running as much as he could for the rest of the game, but now, it seemed like he didn't have a choice. His team's goalkeeper wasn't even looking in the right direction, and the other team was going to score if Massi didn't do *something*. The rest of his team had noticed what was happening and were running down the field, but Massi was so much closer, and he knew he was the only one with a decent chance of getting there in time. He kept running, wincing every time his bad foot hit the ground, speeding up all the same, and eventually drew level with the boy with the ball, snaking his foot around to send it spinning off in the opposite direction – but the other boy had too much momentum, flicking the ball with his foot and sending it right over Massi's leg and into the goal. Their feet caught each other and the other boy, just trying to stay upright, shoved his arm into Massi's shoulder. Massi crumpled onto the ground, his ankle folding up beneath him, finally completely useless.

The next thing Massi knew, Frank, Coach Asher and the rest of the team were all crouching down next to him. "Massi, are you okay?" came Asher's voice.

Massi nodded, and then shook his head, not really sure. "I tripped earlier. I thought it would be alright but-" He broke off, breathing heavily as the pain suddenly got worse. His parents ran up to them as well, concerned for Massi's wellbeing.

"You should have said something, that's why we have substitutes," Coach Asher chastised, and Massi nodded. He hadn't been trying to do anything wrong, he just didn't want to cause a scene.

"Can someone take him back to the clubhouse? Get him an ice pack?" Coach Asher sighed.

Frank volunteered immediately, crying out "I'll do it!" and the next thing Massi knew, Frank was helping Massi to his feet while his parents followed quietly behind.

Despite how much it hurt every time his foot came into contact with the ground, the walk back to the locker room wasn't so tough.

"I'm really sorry, Massi," Frank told him, holding an ice pack to Massi's foot.

Massi was still trying not to cry, and the ice was an unwelcome shock. "Why? You're not the one who pushed me."

"No, an' you know I never would. But I left you on your own down that end. I should have tried to help."

Frank was kneeling on the hard floor of the locker room, and that had to hurt something awful considering how banged up his knees were from the game. "I can hold the ice pack if your knees hurt. You can come sit with me," Massi told him.

Frank thought about it for a moment, and then made a decision. He sat himself on the bench next to Massi while his mother carefully placed Massi's leg over her lap, so she could hold the ice pack in place. She looked proud of him, smiling at Massi, and suddenly Massi's ankle didn't feel as painful as it had.

"You played really good today," John said with a proud smile. His eyes cut to Frank, "You all did."

"Thank you sir," Frank said.

"You were better. You scored three goals. That's amazing." John continued.

"Yeah well it was a team effort."

"Yes you played really well as a team," John agreed.

Frank nodded, smiling.

Massi wiggled his foot in his mother's lap, and Frank reached out a hand to hold him still. "It still hurts?"

"Yeah," Massi screwed up his mouth, unable to deny it, no longer feeling like he had to put on a brave face. "But I don't know what else to do about it."

CHAPTER FOUR:
Development Side

As Massi's skill improved so did his notoriety. One very memorable moment happened when he played at a tournament out of state. When his mom saw the other three teams that Massi's team had to beat she said to herself, "Our team has no chance in front of these tall and well built boys."

By this time of course, Massi had grown into a pretty tall and well built kid at his age too. His skills had also grown with him and made him a player to be reckoned with. He was a team player, interested more in developing the whole team than winning prizes. There were 3 teams to beat in this tournament though, and Melissa was worried. Unlike Massi, she liked to win as much as she enjoyed watching her son play. John was just happy that his son had adopted his love of soccer.

The first game began with a bang and Massi made a run for goal right away. He took the other team by surprise and managed to score their first goal before the opposition could marshal its defense. The second goal was scored by the team captain through a Massi's assist. The other team rallied and managed to score one goal before the match ended.

The second team was even more of a challenge because they'd watched the elementary school team play the first match and had marked all their good players. So now all of the good players including Massi were shadowed by a member of the other team. It was difficult to get the ball let alone dribble. The other team managed to score a goal just before half time. When Massi's team came out of the changing room after a talk with Coach Asher, they were bound and determined to score. They came out with speed and aggression, trying to ditch their shadows. Finally Thomas was able to score through a Massi corner kick. The game ended in a tie.

The third game was the most fun one, the boys were playing good and confident. They won the game 2-0. Thomas, and Frank managed to score one goal each.

The last match was the most difficult. It was extremely intense with both teams not wanting to concede a single goal. The game got rougher and rougher and Massi could hear his mother screaming his name from the stands. Frank lobbed the ball to Massi who was in the midfield and he turned with it, dribbling down the field with determination. Before he knew it he had left everyone behind except the goalkeeper and one defender who was standing outside goal. He kicked with all his might toward the corner of the net and the goalkeeper just missed it. He had scored. On seeing that, the opposing team redoubled their efforts and soon they scored as well. The score was even. In the second half, a body check resulted in a penalty for Massi's team. Thomas came forward offering to take the penalty but he became nervous at how much pressure there was to score.

"Maybe you should do it Massi," he said.

Massi hesitated, also feeling the pressure of not wanting to miss the goal. But he took a breath and decided to take the penalty.

"Come on Massi! You can do it!" he could hear his mother's voice in the crowd.

He put the ball down, stood on an angle taking a running start and kicking the ball in the net, top right with extreme force and precision. The crowd exploded with happiness; Massi's teammates piled on top of him in celebration.

Soon it was back to the game though and nine out of eleven players were now playing defense to make sure the other team didn't equalize. Pretty soon, the whistle blew and the game was over. Elementary school team had won. Everyone was so happy. Melissa and John were jumping up and down with glee. Massi heard someone in the crowd say, "That kid is a crazy player, did you see his kicks?"

He wondered if the person was talking about him.

Soon it was time to collect their prizes and Massi was named Most Valuable Player. He knew he had played well but it was still a huge surprise; a happy one though. They stood in a line while their names were called and each got a gold medal for making first place. Then the individual medals were given out and Massi got his MVP trophy. He held it up for everyone to see and saw his parents cheering. Thomas was standing with the other players, smiling proudly up at Massi. Massi jumped off the podium and walked towards the other players, and held the trophy out to Thomas.

"You should have it." He said.

"No! I can't." Thomas replied.

"You need it more than me. Have it." He said.

His parents came up to him smiling proudly.

"Massi, why did you do that? Why did you give your trophy away?" Melissa asked.

"I play for fun, -*I love soccer*! I don't need prizes; I like to play and win!"

His dad ruffled his hair with pride and his mother beamed.

As they went out for ice-cream after the match, Melissa looked at Massi with proud eyes, "Your kicks are strong Massi... the ball just bombs out from your foot."

"Thanks mom." He replied with a grin."

Coach Asher heard her and came over to their table, "You know Massi, you've got a Magic Foot, the one that you use to score all the time."

Massi just nodded and grinned.

∞

Massi went on to improve in leaps and bounds as his experience with the team continued. He was on his last season. Massi continued to score goals for them, putting his magic foot to good use. They won every match.

On the day of one of their matches, Massi was down with the flu. His fever was running high and his doctor advised bed rest. He still made his dad go for the match so he could record it for him. The team lost that game and it just made Massi determined to get better faster.

When he was cleared to practice again, his team welcomed him back with cheers.

"We're so glad to have you back," they said, "Now we can continue winning!"

CHAPTER FIVE:
Travel Team

When Massi finished elementary school, his coach advised him to try out for the travel team.

"You're good enough to make it. You should totally do it." He said.

Massi was excited about trying out, and very, very nervous. He really wanted to go on to this next phase of his career. He woke up early on the morning of try-outs and did some warm up exercises before he had a healthy breakfast. Then he got on his bike to ride to the try-out pitch.

There were several people he knew trying out including Thomas. Massi wished them all luck for their try-outs before he embarked on his own. They also wished him well.

Massi was excited and pleased to see that he got picked for the travel team after try-outs. It was the best in town and Massi was looking forward to making them proud. The work he had to do was a lot more than on his recreational school team. They had more practices and longer ones; and harder but Massi did not want to miss a single one or be late for any of them. Here he met a lot of very good players, but Massi continued to stand out with his unique talent.

Massi made new friends and his new coach was impressed with his work ethic. He expected a lot more from him than Coach Asher though. Massi was ready to give it to him. He so enjoyed playing, putting his strength against the opposing teams they met. Hearing the roar of the crowds when they scored a goal. They won some games, and lost others because the competition was much tougher. Massi continued to get better as he learned new skills and honed old ones even more. After a couple of years at travel team, Massi's team became one of the best in town.

As we all know in life we face good and bad, and sometimes the bad comes in the area we are most passionate about. One day Massi woke up with his knee bothering him. He had just come back from an away match and was home resting up. He tried to do some warming up exercises but the pain didn't go away.

"Mama," he called limping down the stairs, "There's something wrong with my knee, it's also swollen."

Luckily for Massi, they had good health insurance so his parents were able to take him to the clinic right away. They waited in the reception, Massi between Melissa and John, really worried about what could be happening with his knee because it really hurt a lot. He rubbed at it absentmindedly, wishing for the pain to go away but it seemed to ebb and flow, throbbing in waves of pain. Melissa put her arm around his shoulders to comfort him and he laid his head on her shoulder.

Finally it was their turn to see the doctor and they walked in slowly, Massi limping in between his parents. The doctor examined his knee carefully. Then he sent him down to radiology to get an x-ray. It took a while because there was quite a line but finally they were able to get in to the x-ray room and have Massi's legs x-rayed. After that they went back to the waiting room to wait for results.

It took a while but finally the doctor called them.

"I don't think it's anything serious," the doctor said, "You just need to rest your knee and take some anti-inflammatory medication which I will prescribe for you. Don't worry. You will be fine."

"Really? Oh thank God," Melissa exclaimed with relief.

Massi grinned, "Yeah I was really worried."

"Well…" the doctor said, "That is not all we found."

Melissa, John and Massi all stopped in their tracks, staring worriedly at the doctor.

"What is it then?" John asked.

"The x-ray picked up something else in Massi's bone." The doctor said.

"What?" Massi exclaimed in shock, "What did it show?"

"Massi, you have a bone problem in your other leg," the doctor said gently, looking Massi in the eye.

Massi's eyes were wide open in shock, "H-how bad is it?" he asked.

"Well…it's a bone problem, which means it might get worse with time."

"What's the prognosis?" Melissa asked.

"I can't tell. There is no way to predict what's gonna happen."

"So it might not get any worse?" Massi pointed out.

The doctor sighed, "I'm not ruling it out. We'll keep an eye on it."

"And if it gets worse? I won't be able to play soccer?"

"I'm saying that it's possible that you might not be able to play soccer in the future. But for today, all you need is bed rest and some anti-inflammatories. We will keep an eye on the other situation and see how it progresses."

Massi turned to his mother with distress, "The bone problem is right on my "magic foot" mom," he cried.

Melissa stood up and came to give him a warm hug, "It's okay baby. We'll get through this together."

Massi's father nodded his agreement.

They left the doctor's office and Massi was on bed rest for a few days, taking his pain meds faithfully. Pretty soon the pain in his knee went away and he was able to resume practice. Coach had him on an easy schedule for two weeks, just to make sure he was okay. He thought about telling his coach and his teammates about what the doctor had said but then decided that since it wasn't a present day reality, he would shelve it for now. If things got worse in the future, then he would tell his teammates and coach about the problem.

He continued to travel with the travel team, scoring goals and being a team player. His leg didn't give him any trouble so far and he decided that he was going to enjoy playing soccer while it lasted. His parents held prayers for him every day, keeping watch on his health and learning about all the medical interventions that might exist and that they might have to look into in the future.

But they had faith that everything would be fine with Massi's leg and supported him in his ambition to play for Barcelona or Chelsea one day. He was gaining quite a few fans and followers because of how well he played and being with a team that traveled a lot. He continued to make sure that he was honing his craft, getting as good as he could. He also made sure that his lifestyle was healthy; drinking plenty of water, taking his multivitamins especially calcium and vitamin D, and getting enough sleep. Even with his lifetime of playing soccer, he felt like he was at his healthiest after he learned about his health issue. He learned that a positive attitude went a long way to feeling healthy in his body. He wanted to let other people know, who also had similar diagnoses or were worried about their health, that it was not the end of the world; that they could still live their dreams even if their bodies were not at 100%.

He decided that he wanted to inspire people and use soccer to spread love and also spread love for the game. He credited soccer with giving him focus and purpose and helping him to succeed even in other areas of his life like academics. Soccer helped him make friends, and develop his character and gave him a fun, healthy outlets for all his excess energy. And now soccer was helping him to deal with his diagnosis in a positive way by giving him something to focus on and aspire to.

Printed in the United States
By Bookmasters